WHERE THE WISDOM LIES

A message from nature's small creatures

WHERE THE WISDOM LIES

A message from nature's small creatures

HOPE IVES MAURAN

AuthorHouse™
1663 Liberty Drive, Suite 200
Bloomington, IN 47403
www.authorhouse.com
Phone: 1-800-839-8640

AuthorHouse™ UK Ltd.
500 Avebury Boulevard
Central Milton Keynes, MK9 2BE
www.authorhouse.co.uk
Phone: 08001974150

First published by AuthorHouse 10/2/2006

ISBN: 1-4259-6971-2 (sc)

Printed in the United States of America
Bloomington, Indiana

This book is printed on acid-free paper.

Cover and Interior Design by Legwork Team

CONTENTS

List of Illustrations

Foreword

*T*his is a chronicle of an experience I had in the woods in the spring of 2005; I have not written this book in the traditional sense. I was leaning against a tree that I often visit- when a door opened up within my mind, leading me to a place called 'the Underworld'. Over a period of several weeks, I took my laptop computer into the woods, sat by the tree and visited the Underworld. The small creatures of this place have an urgent message they wish to share with you.

-Hope

Natural Time Vs Artificial Time

My dog, Sunny, and I walk in the woods almost every day. It feels good, clears my mind, and Sunny loves it. Sometimes the birds and the trees communicate with me, so I guess I wasn't as surprised as you might think, when …

On May 17th of last year, I was leaning against a special tree and meditating when right behind me a door opened up. I stood up and turned around. A gnome was standing there. He was short, stocky and red-haired with a thick beard and twinkling eyes. He motioned for me to follow him.

The gnome hurried along so quickly that I didn't have the chance to ask any questions. I felt safe, so I followed him through the open doorway in the tree. The entrance was low and I had to bend down to fit. He led me downward into a dark tunnel. The floor was dirt; the walls were made of stone, roots and earth. We came to a wooden door at the end of the underground corridor that led into a brightly lit chamber. The gnome showed me into the room and left. As my eyes adjusted, I beheld a huge, fat-looking toad sitting there majestically with a crown upon his head.

"Welcome," he said in a baritone voice, his long tongue shooting out.

"Hello," I replied, as I stood up straight in the chamber. Even then, the giant toad towered over me. We looked each other over: I, the thin, fair-haired human; he, the rotund, speckled grey toad. His huge brown eyes seemed to look into my very soul.

"Who are you? What is this place?" I asked as I looked around.

The giant toad towered over me.

"One question at a time, please," the toad said slowly. "This place is called the Underworld, and it is where the wisdom lies. I am the lord of this place."

"Oh," I said, not sure how to respond.

The toad smiled. "You have come here to learn and to bring wisdom out into the world." He certainly seemed sure of himself.

"Yes," I said, surprising myself.

"Then we shall begin with an explanation as to why this must be done now," the toad nodded. "There is no longer time to play around, to dally. The Earth, the fragile pearl and treasure, is failing and she needs to be held in the light by man before it is too late. This Earth is a place of great complexity, yet humanity has no knowledge of why or how she operates. This is what I would like to help you understand so that you may bring this knowing to the Earth's surface and to the places where it may be heard and seen by man.

"It began long ago and the origins may seem unimportant, but there is a wisdom that comes from understanding the beginning." The toad settled himself and continued. "This beginning was an influx or contraction followed by a large explosion. This rhythmic pulsation caused this creation to be born. This spark of life, or Earth, was formed as it gathered the debris of the explosion and still gathers the dust from the cosmos. What this means is that we here on the Earth are not an isolated system. We are not immune to what goes on beyond what we see."

The toad rested for a moment, licked his lips and continued, "When the time came for the formation of the material Earth, the forces in action in the universe focused upon her as a place to create, and play with creation. This is what has been going on here since the beginning of time. This Earth was created as a playground both for creators and the created. All that we have here now is the result of much trial and error. Much time has been spent balancing and blending energies and this has created a delicate web of life and mass that we call the Earth. Are you with me?" The massive toad looked down directly at me.

"Yes, I think so," I answered.

"The start of all of this creation and this intermingling of life and matter was a celebration or a playground… a 'let's see what will happen if…' kind of place. This is what has been going on here, and you, humanity, are the latest on the list of beings that have been living here as *creators*.

"You are coming to the sorry end that many systems of humanity have come to before, all for the same foolish, short-sighted reasons. The reasons are greed, lust, and competition. These things have been the downfall of civilization after civilization. They will be *your* downfall as well, if you don't figure out how to curb them."

I felt a little uncomfortable, as he continued. The toad shook his head sadly, "We often sit in council and wonder how best to help you all. We sit and think, 'Shall we help? Is it futile? Is there any point?' And those of an optimistic bent fight for your cause with great vehemence. So here you sit, lured to this chamber to receive the wisdom of the Underworld, exploring possibilities for ways in which we might work together to create a transformational shift that brings healing forth for all our sakes. So let us get on with it."

"Do you want a chair?" he asked, "This may take awhile..."

"No thank you," I replied.

The great toad shifted his weight to get more comfortable, and began his tale. "Once, time was very different from the way you experience it now on Earth. Your ancestors held a sense of time within themselves that worked in correlation and harmony with nature and the Earth. It was what was, there was no sense of any other way. The rising of the sun, the setting of the sun, the coming of the seasons and the cycles of the moon--this was how time was… and is. It is just that man has separated himself from this natural time and has created artificial time, so that his trains and planes might move on schedule. This is what is causing the downfall of all the Earth systems. This simple and seemingly innocuous shift to artificial time is causing the whole Earth system to fall apart. Never before has this been the reason for the downfall, never before has there been such a time of remorse, and yet so much potential for positive change. For those members of humanity, who see this inconsistency and understand the reason for it, will see clearly what has been done to the Earth and will know that there is no choice but to shift back to natural time."

"What does that mean?" I asked.

"Don't rush me. I will get there," he said, steadily. Gazing off into the distance, he continued, "As I was saying, never before has this difficulty arisen. The problem has become worse in the past one hundred to one hundred and fifty years It is hard to imagine how the "time machine," the clock that man has chosen, could be the cause of the downfall of a civilization that is thousands of years old! It is difficult to comprehend that the power of a system devised to document the passage of time could be so detrimental. Let me explain.

"The Earth is a clock herself; she ticks like a heart. The heartbeat of the Earth holds a steady rhythm that is the harmony of all life at the deepest level. It is what beats in your veins, in your heart and in your meridians. This natural rhythm is the essence of the Earth, and it flows through all that is created of the Earth.

"This is where humanity took a wrong turn. They said, 'we will walk to a different time clock now.' This has created a dissonance that is powerful and growing. This has created a distance from the Earth herself for those who wear the watch. You see, when one wears the watch, one is declaring allegiance to the man-made time system, and one is separating himself from his own, inherent time system. This has repercussions on many, many levels."

I discreetly checked my wrist to see if I was wearing my watch as he continued. "For example, those who wear the watch are declaring that time is of greater import than the rhythm of life. Life does not flow with time; it flows with nature's rhythm. There is winter, the time of quiet regeneration and rest. This is the time when all beings hunker down, examine what is in their lives and slow down to a crawl—find a cozy warm place and be still, as though in hibernation.

"The spring comes and those wearing a watch hardly notice, for the schedule is the same. The spring brings renewal, energy, rebirth and growth, bright new shoots of green spring forth. Eighty percent of plants' growth happens at this time. This brings fresh perspective, ideas, expansion and opportunity to nature and all of life.

"Summer follows, the time of strengthening, of weathering and practice--the time to use energy wisely as it becomes hot and muggy. This is a time of rest, for being together in groups, for travel and communication--for creation together as one.

"The fall is a time for shedding what is unnecessary and of gathering the harvest of that which has grown. This harvest can yield abundance forever, but is dwindling because of the ignorance of humanity in the methods used and the ways of creating food and bringing it to market.

"So you see, my dear," the toad peered down at me, "natural time is the essence of wisdom. Artificial time is short-sighted, damaging, and foolhardy. The Earth is in a dire situation now because of the dissonance humanity creates as it rushes around without the rhythms of the Earth and the seasons. These disparate energies are damaging and fragmenting the Earth Mother, causing systems to fall apart.

"What we see for humanity is one of two things: either the dissonance will continue, ultimately destroying the Earth, or we will see a shift in humanity and its willingness to harmonize with the rhythms of nature and life. Now, what does this mean? You humans have to decide."

Suddenly, the wall behind the toad seemed to dissolve and I was able to make out a large gallery of animals and insects all seated as a council. They were a diverse lot of Underworld dwellers; little furry snout-nosed animals, insects with antennae, lizards, snakes, and more.

"From here, we, the Council of the Underworld, are asking for your help."

I thought to myself, "what can I do? I am just one person."

The toad cleared his sizable throat. "We wish for your help and assistance in bringing this message to humanity. We ask you who dwell in the halls of man, to bring this dissonance to the attention of those who might make the switch. Of course, this requires the complete reworking of time as man sees it, but there really is no choice. Humanity must shift to a natural clock to head off the dissonant fragmentation of the Earth herself. This is really so simple and clear that there is not much more to say on it. You may ask questions if you wish."

I looked at the assembled council and asked, "What are we not getting or giving by using the clocks we have now?"

"When systems work together, it is like all of the clock pendulums in a room are entrained and swinging together," the toad explained. "If one huge clock's pendulum swings in the opposite direction and is completely out of beat with all the others, eventually the room falls apart, because neither is capable or willing to surrender to the opposing beat."

"What would it look like for humanity to live by the natural clock?" I inquired.

"The natural clock is the clock of the sun, the moon, the stars and the year. It is the harmony of the fresh breeze and the present moment. It is the choice to stay home and not go to school, to cocoon or to play, instead of following the schedule." The toad seemed to smile. "It is the movement with the energies of delight and joy that can come when a set schedule is not imposed by government rule. In fact, it is this system that is government ruled that is causing difficulty. Even if one chooses the natural clock, one is called to task for artificial time posts that come each year. They come not on a set day, but a set date. The stars are not aligned for tax day. Holidays are imposed and artificial." All the animals in the council nodded their agreement.

"This is the crux of the issue; this is the dissonance that is damaging. When the systems cross and don't *fully* harmonize, it is an irritant. If the heart of a baby had two beats that were not synchronized, the baby could not grow. It would just exist. We are now in just that same place here on Earth, thanks to humanity," The toad looked deeply into my eyes, as if pleading with me for understanding. "Your generations have caused a discord of magnificent proportions and this shift must come in order for *all* life forms to grow and to evolve. We offer you this information so that we might not all be held back from the evolutionary growth that has brought us all to this point in time. Why let one silly misstep ruin the whole creative experiment? Why?" The great toad sighed heavily. "'*Why not?*' you may say. Agh..."

The toad blinked a few times, and then continued, more optimistically, "When humans see this, there will be fabulous shifts that bring a whole new level of life and harmony to the entire Earth." He folded his hands in front of himself "With that, enough has been said today. We ask you to return here again for additional information that will assist you in your task. You may go now."

I cleared my throat, trying to find my voice. "Thank you," I said, and backed out of the chamber.

The gnome was waiting patiently for me and walked me back up towards the surface. I could see the light of a brilliant sunset in the distance. The little gnome glanced back, smiling, and there was a mischievous glint in his eyes. He started to say something, then seemed to think better of it, turned and scurried up the path to the light. He left me outside the tree, nodded in farewell, and was gone.

I stood there for a moment and thought to myself, "Did that really just happen?" Yet the message made sense. I walked through the woods feeling a bit light-headed. Sunny was racing back and forth, happy to be moving again.

A door opened in the side of the tree.

We Need Your Help

I walked to the tree and sat for barely a moment. The gnome appeared just as before in the open door of the tree. He led me down into the dark without a word. I touched the walls of wood and rock and earth. The tunnel was wet and drippy in places. Finally, we came to the chamber. Again it was brightly lit, although I couldn't see where the light was coming from. The toad was waiting for me, with a smile on his great face. "Welcome back, my child."

I smiled back. "Thank you."

"Let us continue with our story," he began "As humanity has chosen the path of artificial time and of disharmony with the Earth rhythms, there are fewer and fewer options for the Earth. The fragility of the systems is ever-increasing. This means that there is no other way to progress than to break down and rebuild. When a house is no longer sound, the simplest thing is to tear it down and start over. This is what our Earth is considering as her next step. But this is not the desire of all the kingdoms. You see, this is why we have enlisted your help to prevent this extreme course of action, this debacle reorganization from being enacted. Man must learn. Man must know. Humanity's options are limited… May we suggest a reorganization of the way you live?"

The toad gazed off in the distance as if to focus his thoughts. "We shall bring forth our wisdom and ideas for your review and possible use. They carry much potential to be useful and constructive." The council of animals behind him all nodded their approval. "What this means is that we are offering our services and will give some possible solutions through you. If you are interested in receiving them, that is." He looked down at me with his large, penetrating eyes.

"Yes," I stammered at once. "I would like to hear what the council suggests."

The great toad smiled with genuine affection. He cleared his throat before continuing, "There are a few...shall we say, 'stipulations', that are necessary before we continue."

"And what would those be?" I ventured.

"Number one, we must have your word that you will give this information out to the world, and that it will be heard." The toad waited for my answer.

"I will do what feels right," I hedged, "yet it seems that your message is important. It is my hope that I can spread your words."

The toad seemed to approve of my answer. "Secondly, you must find the time to come to this place often enough to get out all the information that is required."

"How much information?" I queried. "How long do I need to be here at a time?"

He turned to confer with his council before answering, "An hour daily should be enough, for perhaps... a fortnight."

"Some days I might not be able to make it," I started to explain apologetically. "But I will get here fourteen times if that is what you require."

"Yes." The toad clapped his hands together. "Thank you for your agreement to our terms." He cleared his throat and smiled his approval to the council before continuing, "At a time such as this, there are many choices. The most obvious of which is to bury one's head in the sand. This is not the best option" he said dryly. He looked down his nose at me to see if I agreed.

I nodded.

"We must have other solutions, and this is where my brethren have been very helpful." He looked to his right at the assembled council "They are filled with ideas and are eager to assist as the days move ahead. On your next visit you will talk with the weasel." A glossy brown animal with a black tipped tail stood up and came over to me. The weasel didn't come too close; he appeared to want me to recognize him and wanted to get a good look at me as well.

The toad went on, "The animals will come forth one at a time to give you their ideas, and we will end afterward with a summary. Is that acceptable?"

"Yes, that sounds fine." I smiled at the weasel.

"That is enough for you today," the toad winked. "We will see you again tomorrow." With that he nodded at the gnome who ushered me back up the tunnel again and out into the daylight.

Sunny was waiting there by the tree for me, and we continued our walk as I wondered where all this might lead.

The Earth is Alive

*T*he weather was getting hotter on this first day of June. I sat under the special tree as usual and the door opened once more. The gnome nodded to me and smiled, holding the door for me. As I passed inside the tree, he turned and led me down into the cool tunnel. We ended up in the great subterranean chamber where the Lord Toad was waiting. He offered me a slight smile and a nod before beginning.

"I see you have come as planned. We thank you and ask that we begin right away." The toad gestured to the weasel, who was already out of his chair and coming forward.

This weasel was larger than one would expect, just like the toad. She was slender, upright and a bit nervous. She bowed to me before speaking in a thin, squeaky voice, "I wanted so much to meet you. You have no idea... Well..." she continued, realizing this wasn't the topic and that the toad might become impatient. She glanced up at the toad before hurrying on, "What I... so wanted to tell you about, is the need for awareness and greater understanding of the little animals and the wee ones that inhabit the Earth. When you bigger folk do things, you make it so we can't do what we need to do. We mix the mulch layer and create the scurry and movement that is required at this level. We are the tenders of the skin of Mother Earth. We mix and improve what lies on the ground. When we can't do this, the Earth loses circulation."

The weasel offered a slight smile, almost seeming embarrassed. "Circulation is critical for her skin's vibrant health. You see, the Earth is living —every square inch of her—and our job is to tend to these small areas that are primarily beneath your sight. We help the Earth to be strong because she can feed her deeper levels when the surface is well cared for, ever-changing and permeable. This is the reason why we are upset and frustrated by humans who don't notice this important work that we do, and want to continue to do."

The little weasel looked up at me, shyly. "Does this make sense to you?"

"Yes, of course." I said. "What do you suggest?"

"I think if people could consider the needs of the little animals to do their work, it would be a big help to us. Like not scraping away all the soil and reshaping what there is, but to leave it like it is and use it as gently as possible."

The toad looked down at the weasel as if to encourage her to continue.

"Well, really, that is all I have to say. All of this is on the collective mind of my brethren, that we be able to do our scurrying work and moving energy of the realms close to the ground. That is all." With that, the weasel looked down at the ground and shuffled off like a shy school child.

Toad and I looked at each other, and he cleared his throat. "I think that is enough for today. We appreciate your coming and look forward to your return. Thank you."

The gnome took me up the tunnel and left me at the door with a nod. It had started to sprinkle. The rain felt good, falling lightly on my arms. I breathed in scent of the wet earth as it started to rain harder and Sunny and I ran for the car.

We are tenders of the skin of Mother Earth.

Animals Need a Place Too

The door opened and there stood the gnome. With a twinkle in his eye and a gentle laugh he motioned to me and said, "Come on now." It was the first time he had spoken to me. He scurried along ahead of me, down the tunnel in the tree. I bent over, following him, noticing how the mica sparkled in the rocks. I saw the light of the chamber ahead. The door opened to admit me and there in the bright light, the toad was waiting.

"Greetings, wee one. We welcome you here to the Underworld," he said with a bit of pomp.

"Thank you."

"Are you well?" he asked.

"Yes I am, although busier with these visits down here."

The toad smiled, "You will be fine." He glanced back to the council, and an animal came forward, eager, yet tentative at the same time. "This is the stoat," the toad informed me.

The stoat stood up on his hind legs, fiddling nervously with its forepaws. "What I want to say is this," he began. "You humans are all so greedy, it seems. You aren't able to let the others of us have their fair share of this life. And we stoats want you to stop doing this so we can just live. What happens, you see, is that many of us are killed and sent away when there is 'improvement', as you call it. We stoats, and lots of others like us, are sent off to find our way someplace new. We realize that you do not do this to us on purpose, but you don't see us or know we're here and so that's what happens. What you need to let the other humans know is that there are lots of animals and they need a place to live too. You see, we are all different. We all like different places, and finding places that work for all is real nice. This is what I need to say to you, and I am hoping you're hearing it. Thank you." The stoat bowed and scurried back to the council seats. His council members applauded politely and he bowed back to them with a bit of embarrassment.

"That's it for today." said the toad. "Thank you for coming, dear," He seemed a bit emotional when he added quietly, "We are really most grateful."

Our eyes met and I nodded and turned to go. The gnome led the way back to the surface and as we stepped out of the tree he said, "So, there it is." And he closed the door behind him

A caterpillar on a silken thread landed in front of me. A spider was weaving a web nearby, and ants were busy with their coming and going. Sunny was busy digging a pit to sleep in. I felt calm and serene as we just sat on Mother Earth and I wondered at the life that was all around me.

The Beetles Die

The door opened behind me. The gnome was there, bidding me to enter. He moved quickly ahead and downward. I touched the walls and the little gnome waited patiently for me. The door to the council chamber opened into the bright light. The toad was there, unmoving, and fast asleep. I touched him gently to awaken him. He pretended to clear his throat to cover his dozing. "Good morning! A-hem…we shall begin. Today we have a special treat for you. A beetle named Jackson will come forward now."

A basic black beetle about a foot and a half tall, slipped out of his chair in a childlike way. It reminded me of a student being called up to the blackboard to write out a problem in math class. He nodded to me and began. "You see it's like this: the world that we beetles live in is very different from your world. It is because we are so small and limited to the very inches above and below the ground. There is a lot of stuff that we can't be a part of. When the inches of ground just above and below us are not available or are destroyed, then there is simply nowhere for us to go. It is a very sad thing that happens, because what the beetles do then…is die. And there are not enough of some of us anymore to make up sustainable populations. We see you all come with your maps and your bulldozers, and we see you dig and change and plop down your houses and your shopping malls and your roads, and we move over, and over, and over again. Mostly, though, we die. All of the beetles die when you move the earth around. Some of us get away, but most do not. So, what happens is that the beetles that live in any area of 'development' are being destroyed, and that is the story of our world. Now, we know you probably have a story too. And we are happy to hear that now."

"You are right," I said to the beetle. "We are taking so much of your land, and I agree, we don't think of you beetles, because you are so small. Sometimes we think of the larger animals, but mostly, you are completely right. We see the land, and we only evaluate it in terms of other humans, not thinking of animals, insects, worms, weasels, stoats, nature, or the Earth. We have kind of forgotten the interconnectedness of all living things. We have some laws, but our laws are only for the issues we know about, like water pollution, soil erosion, plant loss and such. Humans are rather paradoxical, for in our hearts, we want to be connected with nature and you other inhabitants, yet we don't know how to do this anymore, and have become afraid of you. Please, forgive us I am deeply sorry, and apologize on behalf of we humans who have been ignorant of your presence and needs."

The beetle responded, squirming a bit. "What I hope is that as more people learn about us, they will find ways to let the beetles live. Let them live in peace without the troubles of big equipment and losing the land." He turned and walked deliberately back to sit in his place at the council.

The toad was dozing again and I was wondering what would happen next, when another council member stepped forward in a rush. "I just can't wait a moment longer," it exclaimed. It was another beetle, the same size as the first, sporting large claws and impressive armor plating. "I just can't wait to tell you how difficult it is now being an animal, plant, or insect on this world. Everything has changed; everything is being touched by humanity. All those people are like a flock of locusts. They eat all, so there is nothing left. You don't share what you have, and…" he started to weep. "And it is so cold and barren in the ground in so many places. There is no place to be warm and secure in the winter. In fact, so many of my cousins and sisters are dead now," he sobbed again, "that it is very hard for me, very hard." The beetle produced a large handkerchief and blew loudly into it.

"So…so please," he cried, "please, see what you can do." And with that, he scurried back to his seat and sat down, sniffling a bit. The other council members murmured and tried to comfort him.

The toad awakened with a start. "Have we finished?"

I bowed soberly. "Yes. Thank you very much."

"Then you may go,"

I turned away from the council and the door opened before me. The gnome was waiting there, seemingly amused again. He seemed to like it when humans got a dressing down. We walked up the path to the doorway in the tree. Once I was outside in the light of day once more, the gnome closed the door behind me. I was aware of an uncomfortable pressure in my head and felt the need to walk a bit. Sunny tore off ahead of me, happy to be running free.

The Land is Sacred

 *S*unny was panting while happily digging a hole to lie in. The door in the tree appeared and I left her to her digging. The gnome nodded the way, and we proceeded down the damp, tunnel. He opened the rustic, wooden door to the council chamber and there sat the great toad, as large and grand as ever. We startled him awake. "Greetings, little one. Thank you for coming again. Today we have a treat for you: you will meet the lizard of the glade and den who speaks very softly, but with great sensitivity and wisdom."

The lizard walked towards me, appearing larger than I had imagined. He was almost as tall as me and bright green with a black stripe down his back. I turned to him respectfully.

"We of the Lizard Clan are very saddened by the turn that humanity has taken as of late. The disrespect and the disassociation from the Earth creatures have hit a very high peak. Often, the human is sensitive at least, and responsive to Earth and her little animals, but recently it doesn't seem so. There have always been the young ones who have trapped and tortured the beings called lizard, but now it is different. There is a disregard and an aggressiveness never felt before by our kind We suffer greatly for this and for the difficulty of finding habitable, undisturbed places to simply be as we are. Lizards require a purity of place that most other animals do not because of our skin's sensitivity to light and the rays of the sun."

The lizard looked deeply into my eyes. "Offering our guidance to you here and now, we would say to humanity:

Learn the ways of the land that you live on. Even more importantly, keep it sacred and soft in your heart. Live as though the land cared for your actions. Offer a part of your light and your delight to the animals and nature around you. Never offer your hardness, but only your sweetness to the Earth and the animals that she harbors.

"Often it seems that there are no solutions for humans who are stuck in the places they live. But there *are* solutions for humans. There are always ways to find a new home when you can walk and ride. That is not so with the lizard and other beings of Earth. We have no road maps to tell us where to go. We have no apartment buildings to live in when land gets tight. We have no way to survive when our land is taken.

"We live closely tied to humans in so many ways. It is our great privilege to be as we are now, serving as counselors. We live as One when we live as the light demands. We offer to you our love and wisdom in the hope that you will find the answers you seek. And 'hang ten', as the comic lizards would have me say."

I looked to the toad and he gestured towards the doorway. "You may go now."

I thanked the lizard and left through the door, catching the gnome off guard. He rose from his chair and scurried ahead of me up the tunnel toward the light of day.

As I emerged, a large bird burst out from behind a nearby rock and soared up and up into the clear blue sky.

The Creatures' Play

*T*he door opened behind me. The gnome stood silently, holding it ajar. No expression was discernable on his face and one hand played with his long, red beard. We went down into the dark tunnel under the tree. He burped loudly and giggled good-naturedly, changing the atmosphere as we reached the bottom and opened the council door. The toad woke up upon our entry. "Greetings, dear one. Thank you for your loyal and regular appearances here. We are waiting for you today with some anticipation, for the council has created a presentation for you."

Instantly, a chair appeared before me. The bright light in the room dimmed and the council room suddenly reminded me of a theater stage. A curtain dropped down and an otter holding a script stepped out center stage. He began, tentatively, "Today we would like to present to you a reading and enactment of the life we live down here in the Underworld. We will follow this with a question and answer period for your convenience." He looked up and the curtain lifted to reveal a beetle, a weasel, and a worm on the stage.

The beetle began. "Today we are walking along, taking care of our own work and business. So much to do, so much to do," he said cheerily. "All of these leaves need mulching, all this dung needs filtering, and all the work must get done, must get done."

The weasel looked at a paper list he held in his paw. "Let me see now...hunt the crayfish at the pond...check! Observe the baby quails in the glen...check! Capture two frogs for breakfast... check! Let me see, let me see." He looked up at me. "So much to do to keep the balance of nature's life in the small realms, in the light places and in the dark. So much to do!" He wandered offstage.

It was the worm's turn next. A spotlight followed its slow wriggling across the stage. It made unintelligible, (at least to me), mumbling noises as it went. I could feel the eyes of the council members watching the worm as it continued its odd mumbling until, at last, it wiggled off stage and the curtain came down. I clapped my hands, but the sound was hollow and silly in my ears, so I stopped. There was a scraping of movement from behind the curtain. After a moment, the curtain lifted again. The narrator otter, with stiff whiskers lifted his arms to me. "Offering our world to you is our goal as we send you these messages. Our world is small. It is literally beneath your feet. What do you think of this world?"

With a loud squeak, the spotlight turned and blazed right in my eyes. I raised my hand to shield my vision. "I don't think of it much, except when I come here or compost, or hike or see one of your brethren. When I see them, then I am reminded of your presence and your numbers. You are very important to the creation and destruction of matter on Earth."

The council members cheered, "Yes! She's got it!"

"Very well then," the narrator otter announced, "We would like to continue."

The spotlight swung away from me to take in three animals filing out onto the stage. The worm, the weasel and the beetle stood in a row, with the worm standing as straight as possible for a worm.

"We know of your indifference to our world, and your indifference to your own in some ways," the weasel began. "We would suggest to you and humanity, that this is now a teaching time where those who *know* teach those who don't...all about the Earth and the Underworld. This would mean sharing the knowledge of what we do, how we do it, and our preferences and requirements for living. Practical information to assist you to know us and to help us. And we, in return, will continue to assist you by recycling and rebuilding the earth and the plant mulch in the soil. You humans will never need to do this yourselves; we do it all. Can you imagine if you needed to do our work for us? You will learn to respect us and we will be allowed to do our work unmolested. Is this agreeable to you?"

"I am not here representing humanity," I stammered, "but I see your point. The work you do is critical to humanity and to nature."

"Yes," the weasel declared, pulling himself up to his full height. "We think so, too." Proudly, he left the stage.

The narrator otter spoke from the wings, "This concludes our performance today. Thank you." The curtain dropped with finality. I clapped my hands again. The sound, though still a bit hollow, felt right somehow. I turned back to the toad who turned his head to examine me.

"What do you think?" he inquired.

"I see more clearly the importance of the creatures' work here. I understand that you are all an essential part of the process of breaking down the old that then allows new things to grow and prosper."

The toad nodded. "We would like you to speak for a short while with the caterpillar."

A pudgy white caterpillar with fur walked on many legs out from the council, as tall as a cat, but much longer. "Hello there," it said in a high and sweet female voice. "We would like to share the journey of the caterpillar with you from our perspective. We begin as an egg, then we hatch and eat and crawl, and become like this. Our journey takes us up and down bushes and grasses as we look for specific plants to eat. We find them, and eat, then withdraw into the chrysalis where we are transformed into butterflies. This is our journey, but in some lands, the plants we need are gone. The fields no longer grow, the hot tarmac bakes us. We must not get caught in these lands, for they fry us and we die. My wish for you is to leave the forest as it is, the fields open and un-mowed. Please, honor the land so that we might live and transform into butterflies that grace the earth, like flying flowers. This is what we require. This is how it might be yet again."

"That is all for today," the toad informed me. "You may go now. Thank you so very much for coming."

It seemed to me that the great toad and I were becoming quite friendly. I thanked the animals of the council and followed the gnome as he scurried up the tunnel.

Being in the woods was like being caressed. It was a blessing to see the little creatures everywhere, birds and insects of all kinds, all parts of the natural world through which I normally walk so blithely and take for granted. I was filled with appreciation and love for this interconnected system and these innocent creatures. As was illustrated in the play they had performed for me, we are all players on the stage of Mother Earth and their's is a major role.

Don't Kill Snakes

*T*he door opened behind me and the gnome was there, mopping his brow from the blast of hot air on the surface. He turned and strolled down the tunnel as usual, leading the way down the dark pathway to the toad. We came to the council chamber door, where he stopped me before opening it. "I want to warn you…today's speakers aren't all as nice as those you met last time." The gnome stared at me intensely before opening the door and letting me pass. With his warning ringing in my ears, I took a deep breath, and stepped inside.

The toad was there, looking self-satisfied and still, as though he had been deep in thought and had been interrupted by my entrance. He cleared his massive throat. "I am glad you have come, for we have a special visitor here today who would like your ear. We have told him of our project and he is eager to add his wisdom to the pot, so to speak. He is the snake."

With that introduction, a large snake, who came up to my waist, glided into view, bringing with it that strange and eerie serpentine energy. It felt delicate but powerful; not filled with evil intent, but not to be trifled with. "Hello," he hissed, his tongue darting outward.

I swallowed hard, bowed slightly and answered, "Hello." In my mind, I was wondering about the wisdom of attending this meeting.

"I am s-s-s-so glad you have come," the snake hissed, gazing at me with its laser-like eyes. "I am really s-s-so pleased to meet you. But I must tell you, your kind is a rather unreliable and nasty sort. Not the kind one brings home to meet Mama," he continued with disdain. "You are difficult to coexist with. You see, we are residents and denizens of the lands that are between. We live in the same places that the small animals inhabit, between and betwixt, not here or there. We eat the furry animals that live where we do.

You create imbalance in areas that are none of your business when you kill snakes.

The problem comes because you and your kind are so easily led to believe it is your business and your right to kill my kind. This is not the case. This is very unfair." The snake's voice trembled for the first time. "Your kind takes my life with shovels and sticks and all manner of unmentionable items. And this disturbs the balance for the furry animals that live where we live. They take over because they are not killed so easily and joyfully by your kind. You create imbalance in areas that are none of your business when you kill snakes. Would you have the furry animals overrun your world? This is what you attempt when you kill the snakes you see."

The snake's tongue flickered at me as if to question my motives. Gathering his composure, he continued. "You see, this matters because rodents and other furry creatures carry disease. Your kind will suffer the negative consequences of killing my kind so freely. When these vermin bring their diseases to your lives and your bodies, you shall s-s-see. You shall s-s-see," the snake hissed with obvious relish. "What we would like to suggest is that you send out the message to all other humans: 'No more snake-killing or you will pay the price with your own lives.' This is a choice you now have," he finished and looked me squarely in the eyes, before slithering away through a low hole in the earthen wall of the council room. The assembled animal council nodded and applauded politely, for they were all slightly afraid of the snake and wanted to show their respect.

The toad closed his eyes to rest, and I opened the door, startling the gnome who had been listening with his ear pressed to it. We walked up through the tunnel and I found myself back in the heat of a summer's day.

Sunny was not with me, but the hole she had dug to lie in two days earlier was still there, so I felt her presence anyway.

Thermodynamics

It was a hot, dry day. The air was still and the woods were quiet, but for the sound of a few birds calling. The gnome came to open the door in the tree and I followed him down into the cool darkness of the tunnel. The cavern was a relief from the hot day above ground. He led me to the council chamber without a word.

The great toad opened his eyes to see me and cleared his throat. "A-hem!" he boomed in a commanding tone, "Hello, and welcome to the Underworld!" Then, in normal voice, "We wish for you to relax with us today. To be a bit less formal, we would like to hear from your perspective what this dialogue is about. This will help us to mold it more effectively as we complete it in the next few days."

I felt a little 'put on the spot' as I began. "The Underworld's inhabitants are communicating what they do as part of the living earth system. Keeping the leaves mulched, and the rodents in check, assisting soil structure and aeration. They are upset when man disrupts the Earth for the loss of life is great for the inhabitants who have nowhere to go to live in peace and to do their work...."

The toad lifted his head and smiled wearily. "My dear, I see that we need to get a more in-depth awareness through to you. What you must know is that there is a heart- knowing that is present in our world, and simultaneously, a great wounding of that knowing." I wilted at this thought as the toad continued, "It is because of the insensitivity of *humankind*. Ironic word, no?" he paused. "Because of this wounding, there is little resiliency in the systems and relationships of nature. They feel hopeless and lacking in the necessary energy to sustain the future that is shared by all here on this earthly plane. This kind of depression is biologically unhealthy. It shuts down the systems that maintain adaptability in the face of adverse weather conditions. It renders them energetically isolated. The systems are not building energy between each other in the way they used to. They are becoming weaker and increasingly separated which is the concern and the difficulty.

"We are deeply hopeful that with this information, a spark shall be lit to allow humans who act from ignorance to see clearly. The flame of light and wisdom will be lit for humanity."
With that, the toad turned to the council, and a large claw-armed beetle stepped forward to speak. The creature was bright iridescent green. It clicked when it walked. "Hello there, little lady," he greeted me with kind of an accent that I swear made him sound like a cowboy.

"Hello," I replied, smiling.

"Well, ya see, what I wanted to say to ya is this…" He scratched himself. "There's this thing called thermodynamics. This is when the Earth's energy and warmth are transferred outward to the surface and we inhabitants have the chance to partake in that warmth as a matter of course. Reproduction and all. Well, ya see, this thermo-dynamics, or the movement of the heat energy from the core thermal, is having problems. What's goin' on is that there's this amazing undercurrent that has just come in, and it is undercutting what happens at the surface. Now what this means for you and me, little lady, is that there is a problem brewing. Ya see, this thermal heat energy that comes from the core is different somehow; it's not getting' here. Some places are real hot and some are real cold. It's strange. We have checked in with the powers that regulate this stuff and they don't have any real good answers for us, so the problem we're looking at is kinda huge and scary, and maybe bigger than all of us. But me and my buddies, we think we know why this is going on. We think it's because of the thermodynamic sink that is appearing in parts of the Earth where the energy is being sucked inward, like there's a black hole or somethin' we can't see. There's this strange disappearance of energy, like it's being sucked somewhere else. Now we just wanted you to know of this and be thinkin' of some other plans, 'cause we are sure stumped down here. Got it?" He looked up at me quizzically.

I nodded. "I guess so, but the problem seems a bit large for me to offer much help."

"Simply wanting to help makes us real grateful." He saluted me with his claw and clicked his way back to the council.

The toad looked at me, "That will be all for today. We will see you tomorrow." He waved to the gnome, indicating that it was time to escort me back to the surface. It certainly felt to me that the stories and the problems the animals were presenting were getting bigger. I stopped walking through the woods to say a prayer for the Earth.

"Thank you for the wisdom that shines forth from the animals and the Earth. Thank you for Man's openness in receiving this wisdom. Amen."

Machinery and the Earth

It was hot and dry again. Sunny was panting and trying to dodge the biting fly that was after her. She was happy to be out in the woods again. The door opened, the gnome nodded a greeting, and we went down into the cool and damp. The council room door opened to admit me and the toad awoke. "Greetings, Earth-dwelling human. What is your name, anyway?"

"It is Hope," I answered.

"Ah. Perfect." He smiled with satisfaction.

From the hole in the wall that the snake had disappeared into, a hedgehog appeared. Small, bristly, and cute of face, the hedgehog spoke in cultured tones. "Greetings to you, dear human. I am pleased and honored to be here speaking with you and wish to thank you deeply for your gracious willingness to communicate with our world. With the advent of the automobile, the watch, mechanical farming, and machinery, much happened to the Earth. It has not all been beneficial. I am concerned, for there has been an increasing disregard for the Earth, the animals, and the systems of nature while at the same time there has been an increasing misguided belief in humanity's role as ruler of this planet. When the Earth was formed and much of the life that is here now evolved, there was cooperation and respect. It did not mean that we refrained from eating one another, but it meant that we ate as we were hungry and did not take more than we needed. The difference now is that man feels entitled to take anything he wants, anytime and without recompense. This is terribly sad." The hedgehog looked down with dismay. "We wish to point out this inequity and urge the human family to reconsider and modify these attitudes. This message is a deep opening into the world of the animals and what you call the Underworld. What is happening now is terribly important, and must be examined and re-evaluated as a trend that humanity is choosing. We are offering this gift to you with our deepest and fondest 'hope'..." He smiled for using my name, "that all will resolve itself in complete harmony and joy, even if it means some slight discomforts when choosing different ways of doing things than you have done before. That is really all I have for you. I give you my love and thank you for your willingness to assist us in this way." The hedgehog smiled sweetly.

"It is my pleasure," I responded with a nod, "I too hope that we will find the harmony and respect that you describe for us all here."

The little hedgehog waddled gracefully off back through the hole in the wall through which he had come.

"Do you see how important this work is for us?" the toad boomed. "This information must come out so it can be seen by humans in order to help all the animals, birds, insects, fungi, and each of the interrelated systems so that all may partake of the bounty and joy of this land. For none will survive without the others. You know this, don't you? Many will not survive on Earth without the active and willing participation of the kingdoms that you so carelessly overlook now. Let this be a warning," he declared, raising himself to his full height.

I paused for a moment, reflecting on his words. "Let us create in ourselves the feeling of harmony and balance that we would like to experience, right now and then think of the Earth," I guided. I invited the toad and the council to close their eyes and practice this method of creation with me.

"What does this do?" the toad asked after he opened his eyes.

"It's a way to create with intention," I told him.

"Well, why on Earth isn't all of humanity doing more of it?" he muttered to himself with a sigh. After a few more moments of peaceful concentration, the toad opened his eyes and smiled. "That felt quite lovely. That is quite enough for today. Good day…Hope."

The gnome had been dozing on the other side of the door. I startled him as I opened it to leave. He walked up the tunnel with me and bid me farewell.

On my way home, I reflected on all that had occurred. Sometimes it had been hard to listen to these sweet animals, for I saw their point so clearly, and I knew of the difficulty that lay ahead for all of us, should they be right. There was so much to think about and to reconsider in how our lives are lived. It was as if we had only seen a fraction of the true reality, and now that we had been offered a clearer picture, we had some big choices to make.

Humans are Gone

I arrived at the tree and the door opened instantly, not even giving me time enough to catch my breath. The gnome beckoned me to come, turned and walked into the dark. It had rained the day before and the tunnel walls were dripping.

I found the toad sleeping, but he quickly opened his eyes, cleared his throat and greeted me warmly. "Welcome, my dear. You are always welcome here." He stretched his shoulders back, puffing out his chest before beginning, "Let us carry on. The wonderful thing that awaits us today is a presentation and a question and answer session with the one and only...barking dog spider! This dog spider gets his name from the fact that his face is like a dog's, and it makes a noise, something that no other spiders do."

A furry, light brown spider skittered up to me, legs everywhere, like a daddy long legs but coordinated and muscular. He came up to my waist, which by now seemed quite normal.

"I am ready, dear spider." I bowed.

"Thank you," it cooed in a voice that was unexpectedly tender and sweet given its fierce looking body. "I am so pleased to be able to

There is a strong message that must be given now.

speak to you. This is really exciting. You see, humans are a mystery to us. We don't understand you, what you do and why. It makes no sense to us, so we are wondering what you are all thinking. I should just ask you questions; that would be more interesting for us." The spider turned to the council for agreement. Most agreed with him. "So, let me ask you a few questions."

"Okay," I replied.

"When people try to do something with the Earth, why is it so important to change the ground?" the spider asked curiously.

"I think lots of times it is so that automobiles can drive over the earth on roads that are smooth and flat and not too steep. Or the ground is changed to create a level place for buildings. The land gets moved to accommodate new development rather than having architects design buildings so that the Earth does not have to be disturbed. "

"Oh," the spider said, a bit disappointed. "So why do people feel this automobile is so important? Why does it rush around so?"

"The car is how people get from place to place. They like to move fast and travel far easily, and they have gotten very used to this freedom. In the old days, the horse and buggy or their feet got them where they needed to go. Now people are getting farther and farther away from home more often, and that means not only cars, but also planes and trains rushing around. It is something people don't even notice they are doing."

"Oh my, this is worse than I thought. So tell me this!" the spider exclaimed, "Why are there so many people now? There didn't used to be so many."

"People live longer than they used to. More babies are born and more people survive because of science, food production, and medicines."

"Hmm." The spider seemed perplexed. "There must be some good news from you people. Can you think of anything?"

"Yes, actually," I said. "The good news is that more and more people are living with an awareness of the interconnectedness of all life. There is positive change going on, but it is not happening so you can see it easily without looking for it."

"So, what are these people doing?" the spider asked eagerly.

"They are choosing to live more gently on the Earth. They are respectful to the animals and plants. They thank the Earth for what she gives.

They teach children the importance of nature, and the interconnectedness of all life. They work at jobs that are helping people to live lightly and more consciously upon the Earth. They are doing lots of things; I can't possibly describe them all to you." I waited for the council to digest all of this.

"Hmmm. Okay…I can see there is much to be optimistic about, if what you say is true. Thank you," the spider replied cheerfully. "What I want to say is this: you are the representative chosen to communicate with us in this manner. We are deeply grateful. Whatever comes of this, we thank you. We also would like to say that there is a strong message that must be given now. The days are numbered, and humanity may be spiraling toward a sad and sorry end that we wish to describe for you in detail. This may be hard for you to hear, but we wish you to receive it without judgment. Just receive…"

I relaxed and took a deep breath, and came fully into my body. "Okay, I'm ready."

The spider began,

"See the land parched and bare. The soil scorched and black. See the earth burning and smoking. See no trace of animal or man. See just the land in smoldering sooty

beingness. The trees, mere stumps, charred and pointed. The land is tired and poor. Fire cleanses and clears the land of the pestilence of human form. And much else goes with it as well. The land is difficult to understand for the animals and insects and plants now. They are in hiding or hibernation in their most quiet form, as seeds, or eggs or incubating in a mother. There is the knowing that the life will spring forth in perfect timing and the land will recover. Humans are gone. The animals awaken, look out from their hiding places, and feel glad. The people are no longer! Hurray! Hurray!" the spider exclaimed. "The people had become so difficult to live with, so prideful and boastful, ignorant and slothful, so thoughtless and ugly. The people had become this, and those who weren't, could not be bothered to shine the light of awareness for those who were not aware. Oh my, this is a sad and glorious picture I see, for there is only the land with some small signs of life. But the land is noble, optimistic, sure, powerful and unconquerable! The land is just that."

The spider's last words were like an epitaph for humanity. It slowly walked back to the council and all in the chamber were silent.

Finally, the toad broke the silence. "So...with that, we send you off, my dear, to carry forth these messages to humanity and thus make the shift of light that is required at this time. We say adieu." I was speechless, because I could understand completely the spider's message, as horrifying as it was. I could also see how grand and powerful the earth would remain, regardless of what happened to humanity.

I bowed, and turned to leave. I let myself out this time and walked up the tunnel slowly, deep in thought. As I stepped out of the tree and into the daylight, Sunny came running by, chased by a flying insect, a game she loves to play. I leaned against the tree and cried, feeling the immensity and hopelessness of this task.

We Are All Interconnected

*I*t was a beautiful day. I tried not to think of the weighty message that I held. It was a message that few would want to hear, let alone act upon. Yet, I had called upon my sense of determination, and I felt optimistic and eager to be ending this adventure soon. I sat down, leaned against the tree, and the door opened.

The gnome ushered me down into the chamber. The toad was there, the gold crown glistening upon his head. "Hello, my dear." He spoke sleepily, opening one eye. "Welcome. Today is a day of great significance, because we are soon coming to the 'summer long day' and we wish to talk about that for a moment with you. This 'summer long day' is the longest period of daylight during the entire year, and as such, is auspicious for those who are of the light. Those whose work is of the light notice these extended summer days. Life is easier, less stressful and there are plenty of things to eat and drink. The hot and dry days have not come; there is abundance and joy afoot. This is wonderful for all on the Earth.

"Offering you our wisdom is a pleasure that I will not reserve only for myself today. We will invite the opossum to join us."

The opossum ambled up, sniffing and coming up close to get a good look at me. I offered a soft "Hello." She continued sniffing, checking me out. She circled around me completely before she spoke.

"Okay," she said finally. I sensed that she could tell a lot by the smell of me. "I am pleased to meet you," she began with great clarity. "We have a message for you, we 'possums. There is change afoot. There are new things that must come if we are all to survive." I was surprised by her frankness and focus. "We see the need for change, yet we are completely confused as to what we can offer. I had hoped to receive some information from my inspection of your essence, but without result. So we will resort to that which we had thought of before, which is this message to humanity:

You must try to change your ways, to be more sensitive and thoughtful, to be more generous and compatible with all that goes on here. Working together is the key! That is what must change. Humans, you must see that we belong together; we are all interconnected... We can help and respect one another. Each creature must work with the others in order for all of us to survive. That's it... We must all survive, and the only way to do that is for us to respect the unseen energy systems that are working to keep us balanced. The connection between us all that must be honored and felt. This is so important! You have no idea!

"It would seem that there are only good things that will come if we continue to communicate in this way, and there are only bad things that will come if we don't make some changes. It is really quite simple. If you draw the line pointing to where we are currently headed, *you will find that we are headed off the edge of a cliff. If you draw the line pointing toward 'Together,' it looks a whole lot different. That is all I have to say."*

The opossum gave me one last sniff and walked in that slightly awkward short legged way back to join the council.

The toad looked down at me and we nodded together. Then in a booming voice, he declared, "We are done here. You may go and return another day for our final wrap-up. Thank you for these visits. We will see you anon."

I bowed my head, left the room and headed up the path, following the gnome. I stepped out of the tree just as Sunny came over the rise to greet me.

The Key

The day was overcast and cool. There was anticipation in the air. As I slowly walked to the tree, I pondered the ending of this adventure. I felt regretful, yet relieved all at the same time. I was open to what would come next, and was wondering how on Earth I might follow through with my pledge to bring these words to the people who needed to hear them.

As I sat leaning against the tree, the door opened behind me once more. The gnome smiled, showing huge white teeth and a sweetness and joy in his eyes that I had never seen before. We walked down the path together. It had become a ritual that we had. We walked as we had so many times before, but today it felt different somehow. The path was packed hard; the walls still sparkled and were dripping in places. The light shone through the cracks around the rough, arched door at the bottom. I nodded to the gnome and stepped into the blinding light.

The toad awoke more quickly than usual, remembering the excitement of this being our last meeting. "My dear," he began formally. "We of the Underworld welcome you, and wish to make you an honorary member of the Council."

I felt gratitude and love for the Toad and all the animals of the Council wash over me as I said "Thank you." I smiled at all those assembled. "I would be greatly honored to join your council." Then I giggled to myself at the thought of an obituary write-up that might include: 'and the deceased was an honorary member of the Council of the Underworld...'

The toad continued, "We have prepared a small token of our gratitude for you. It is the key to the Underworld that is yours whenever you choose to use it." With that, he put a heavy key on a burgundy ribbon over my head. It felt cold and heavy.

I touched the key and said, "Thank you." Not quite sure what more I could say, I held the key up before the council. "I am honored to have visited you these times and to hear your message. I have enjoyed it immensely. Your words are heartfelt and wise, and you are generous in your willingness to address humanity, which has done so much harm at this level. I ask for your continued guidance and encouragement to help us to make this shift that is required. I know it is not easy to wish your human brothers and sisters well, perhaps, but I offer that humans are mostly good at heart, and will hopefully hear your words with open hearts and willingness to look at things in a broader way." The council all nodded and thanked me.

The toad turned to me, "We would like to continue with a summary to bring this all together." The council members approved solemnly.

"Yes," I agreed, "that would be helpful."

"So let us begin," the toad announced in his most dramatic baritone voice. "We will all come forward today and sit in council."

All the members of the council arranged themselves to sit in a circle. The toad sat to my right, and weasel, beetle, possum, snake, spider, ermine, worm, otter and others joined in. I waited expectantly for someone to begin.

The weasel stepped forward to address the group. "It was a approximately one month ago that this endeavor began, with much nay-saying and negative projection from many of our members. We are exposing ourselves in a way that we don't always feel comfortable doing. Our wish is to convey our gratitude for your trust and faithfulness in following through to this end.

"We offer from our point of view that there are several issues that must be addressed and brought to light. The foremost and critical one is the timing of life that humanity has taken on, which has resulted in a very detrimental and ominous tone here on Earth. When humans are ignorant of the rhythms that are within the Earth, the stars, the cosmos, and their own bodies, where is the future to lead them?"

I noticed with surprise that the weasel was wearing a miniature pair of reading glasses, which he removed before continuing, to gesticulate. "This is problem number one. The second problem we see is the necessity for respect and honor of all Earth residents. This respect must come from a willing and open heart in order to bring what is best for all into the future days."

He returned his glasses to his face, and went on. "And we wish to see a greater effort on the part of the humans to ensure that there is balance and harmony in the works that take place on this Earth. The works now are deeply imbalanced. Balancing these works will require focus and an open willingness to do and see things differently." The weasel produced a list and continued.

"The fourth thing here is the understanding that all of us are equally important here on the Earth, equally entitled to do our work; equally necessary to the health of the whole earth system, equally willing in our hearts. This is very important—critical, even--to know and feel this. Remember the beetle's message?" I imagined the Earth with all the leaves and debris piling up without ever being broken down and recycled back into the soil, and quickly saw the validity of this point.

"Now, the fifth issue is that humans need to clean up after themselves more effectively. They can not leave the manufactured debris of lifetimes lying around. It is indigestible and needs to be reduced to its bare elements and recycled by humans, because the natural systems can't take it." The weasel looked around the room, and all shook their heads in approval before he continued.

"And lastly, the sixth thing. It is that there must be an optimism of working together, a joy in the diversity of all. There must be an understanding and a realization that we are all here with our own special gifts that we bring. The weasel to stir up the ground, the beetle to break down the leaves, the worm to mix the soil, and so on. We must all be honored as a key part of the whole. We are all of the same desire and must honor our differences with reverence and vigilance. It appears to us sometimes that humans believe that if it doesn't walk on two legs and have the flesh of your kind, it is not worthy of life! This is a deadly illusion which can persist no longer, for all our sakes. This must be known!"

Equality of All ~ Each is
necessary to the health of
the whole Earth system.

— ⋅⋅⋅ ⋅⋅

Clean Up, Recycle ~
Manufactured debris is indigestible to nature.

— ⋅⋅⋅ ⋅⋅

Optimism and joy in work-
ing together ~ we are all
here for the special gifts we bring.

Timing of Life ~ Awareness
of rhythms in the earth, stars,
cosmos and your own body.

~

Respect and Honor all earth
residents with a willing and
open heart.

~

More Effort towards
balance and harmony
in all earthly works.

The weasel lowered his list and looked up at the council. "I believe this ends our list of demands, or encouragements...whatever you wish to call them." As he handed me the list his voice was drowned in the council's applause and cheers of approval.

"My dear..." the toad looked at me with wide, wise eyes, "Hope." He smiled. "We send you off with this list, and wish with all the wellness we can that you will find a way to bring this message to the world of humans. Our hopes are pinned on you."

As the weight of these words hit home, I consciously called up the feeling of optimistic enthusiasm. A sense of power coursed through me as I felt the optimism in my body, then closed my eyes and visualized humanity and the Earth.

I moved around the council, thanking, shaking hands, bowing and hugging where appropriate until I got to the toad. Though he was towering over me, his gaze was warm and kind. He bent down for me to kiss him on the forehead. Then I turned and walked to the door. The gnome, who had witnessed all the proceedings, had a tear trickling down his cheek. He gathered himself up and nodded for me to come. We moved up through the tunnel. At the top, he hugged me and then hurriedly closed the door, as some mountain bikers stopped a few yards away. The doorway vanished and the bike riders continued on, oblivious of the magic that was all around them.

I sat down against the tree, feeling the embrace of the tree trunk and the support of the Earth beneath me. I touched the key around my neck and smiled, feeling completely still inside.

* * * * * * * * * * * * * * * *

As my thoughts turn to you
who are reading this ,
I smile. Feelings of joy and optimism rise up
and flow through me;

I seed the thoughts of humanity with this
knowledge and remembrance.
And ask that you who are reading
do the same.

I remove the key from my neck and
see that it has changed to gold as I place it
around your neck.
Feel its weight. It is pure gold.
It holds this message
that Nature calls out for us to hear.

* * * * * * * * * * * * * * * *

I stand and go back out of the woods.
What happens now is up to you.

The End